PETS AND HEAVEN

WHAT THE BIBLE SAYS

About our Animal Friends

Rev'd Dr. NEAL OTTO HIVELY

Printed and Bound in

The United States of America

FIRST PRINTING

JULY 2010

ISBN 978-0-9827308-0-5

NEAL OTTO HIVELY

CHAMBERSBURG, PA, USA

PET DEDICATION PAGE

This book is dedicated with heartfelt love and affection to

____

Beloved by this human family and eternally cherished in the loving heart of the Creator God.

by

____

Human Companion

BOOK DEDICATION:

In 2010 our nearly fifteen year old Maltese dog Calee died. We discovered that there was very little in print to respond to serious biblical inquiries about God's loving intent concerning animals. This selected devotional and Scripture summary is offered here to address that purpose.

To all lovers of God's creation, for living things – both plant and animal;

To all who touch the lives of God's special messengers of love and grace, animal-lovers; and to those whose lives are uniquely shaped and blessed in that mutual relationship;

To our Veterinarian professionals for their care and compassion;

To animal hospitals and shelters, SPCA Chapters and all compassionate ones who guard, rescue, protect, heal and safeguard animals and plants;

To our animal husbandry, pharmaceutical and pet food industries - in their worthy dedication and ethical scientific endeavors;

To our dear pets, who forever leave their paw prints on our hearts;

And to all living things, Great and Small – all creatures of our Eternal God.

Neal Otto Hively

Eastertide 2010

Calee

TABLE OF CONTENTS

GOD'S CREATION - INTRODUCTION 7

GOD'S CREATION - OUR MANAGEMENT 12

GOD RESCUES HUMANS AND ANIMALS - THE FLOOD 13

GOD'S FIRST ETERNAL COVENANT – THE RAINBOW 15

GOD COMMANDS ALL CREATION TO REST 17

GOD AND CREATION IN THE PSALMS 19

GOD CARES FOR US THROUGH ANIMALS 21

GOD'S GIFT OF HOPE - THE PEACEABLE KINGDOM 22

GOD'S COVENANT TO ALL CREATION 24

GOD AND ANIMALS IN THE NEW TESTAMENT 25

GOD USES A ROOSTER AS A WITNESS 25

JESUS TEACHES ABOUT GOD'S CARE FOR CREATION 26

GOD'S NEW CREATION 28

CREATURES IN HEAVEN 28

GOD'S PERFECT KINGDOM 29

GOD'S CREATION CELEBRATED IN HYMNS 31

BIBLE LEARNING SUMMARY 34

DEVOTIONALS ABOUT ANIMALS 37

SAINT FRANCIS OF ASSISI – PATRON SAINT OF ALL ANIMALS 37

A PRAYER OF SAINT FRANCIS 38

RITE FOR THE BLESSING OF ANIMALS 38

PRAYERS FOR ANIMALS 40

PRAYERS FOR LOST PETS 41

PRAYER FOR ADOPTING A NEW PET 43

PRAYER FOR A SICK ANIMAL ... 43

PRAYER FOR AGING PETS ... 44

PRAYER FOR A DEAD OR DYING PET ... 45

LITURGY FOR THE BURIAL OF A PET ... 46

PRAYERS FOR CATS ... 48

SAINT GERTRUDE, PATRON SAINT OF CATS ... 48

CAT OWNER'S PRAYER ... 49

A CAT'S PRAYER ... 49

THE CAT'S CAROL ... 50

PRAYERS FOR DOGS ... 51

SAINT ROCH, PATRON SAINT OF DOGS ... 51

A DOG'S PRAYER FOR HIS OWNER ... 51

A POLICE DOG'S PRAYER ... 52

GOD AND DOG ... 53

FOR ALL PETS – "A LIVING LOVE" ... 53

PETS' LOVE ... 55

INDEX OF NOTABLE QUOTES ... 56

INDEX OF BIBLE PASSAGES ... 57

PAGES FOR NOTES OR PHOTOS ... 58 - 59

ABOUT THE AUTHOR ... 60

QUOTE: "If there are no dogs in heaven, then when I die I want to go where they went." – *Will Rogers*

QUOTE: "God will prepare everything for our perfect happiness in heaven, and if it takes my dog being there, I believe he'll be there."
– *Billy Graham*

GOD'S CREATION - INTRODUCTION

Did you ever consider how much our animal friends remind us of the sacred characteristics of God? Our pets are often the first to greet us when we wake up and the last we bid goodnight. They welcome us home and miss us when we are away. They are loyal, playful and loving friends. They ask little and give much. So it is with God – always there for us; wishing us to be all that we are called to be in that holy relationship.

What does the Bible have to say about animals and all the rest of creation? Holy Scripture is mostly God's word to people. There are also many indications that God's affection and care extend to all creation, including the earth, sea and all living things.

There are clear Bible passages that God's care and affection extend to all creation, including our pets.

You who choose to read this probably are a pet owner, an animal lover, a farmer, an ecologist or nature lover. You may have a particular affection for your "best friend" in the animal realm. So it is perfectly natural as a person of faith to ask, "Might we be together again in God's eternity?"

The Bible has a lot to say about God's intent for creation and everlasting regard for all that has been made. In its broadest sense, this book is about Creation Theology as it relates to our pets.

What does the Bible say about animals and heaven? The Bible does not directly give an answer to that question. But, there are clear Bible passages that God's care and affection extend to all creation, including our pets.

The Bible has quite a lot to say about the nature of God, what God's desire is for all creation (including animals and plants) and for humankind. So take heart, read on and hear the word of the Lord – for you and for all creation.

Most of what is presently available on the topic of 'pets and heaven' attempts to reconcile God's promises to humanity with God's intent toward all creation. That's the proverbial mixing apples and oranges. The Bible was not intended to directly deal with that topic. However, **what the Bible does say about our dear pet friends appears to be very clear. The Bible passages will speak for themselves.**

Verses that are italicized are my emphasis. Photos and graphics are in the public domain or purchased expressly for this publication. I offer my sincere apologies for materials whose provenance could not be determined and source credit given.

Scripture text is from the **New Revised Standard Version**.

GOD IS THE LORD OF ALL CREATION: we're all made by the same God, from the same stuff - **Dirt.** At our basic core, beginning and end, we're all the same, made from minerals, water and basic elements. **For more on this topic, please read Ecclesiastes 3:16-22.**

QUOTE: "*...for you are dust, and to dust you will return.*" - Genesis 3:19

The Old Testament **Book of Genesis** begins with God creating everything out of nothing. The first chapters of Genesis do not detail "how" everything was created. The declaration in Genesis is that God did it. God is named as the maker of all that is seen and unseen: universe, stars, moon, earth, light, water, land, plants and all the marvelous living creatures of water, air and land. God made you and your pets; God made us all. The Bible declares that God was pleased, **"God saw that it was good."**

"I can do no other than be reverent before everything that is called life. I can do no other than to have compassion for all that is called life. That is the beginning and the foundation of all ethics."

- Albert Schweitzer

Genesis 1:1-2, 1:21-25

"In the beginning when God created the heavens and the earth, [2]the earth
was a formless void and darkness covered the face of the deep, while a
wind from God swept over the face of the
waters…

[21]So God created the great sea monsters
and every living creature that moves, of
every kind, with which the waters swarm,
and every winged bird of every kind. And
God saw that it was good. [22]God blessed
them, saying, 'Be fruitful and multiply and
fill the waters in the seas, and let birds
multiply on the earth.' [23]And there was
evening and there was morning, the fifth
day.

So God created…every living creature… And God saw that it was good.

- Genesis 1:21

[24]And God said, 'Let the earth bring forth

living creatures of every kind: cattle and creeping things and wild animals of the earth of every kind.' And it was so. [25]God made the wild animals of the earth of every kind, and the cattle of every kind, and everything that creeps upon the ground of every kind. And God saw that it was good."

For more, please read all of Genesis 1:1-25

DEVOTION: Can you see God's creative hand, loving care and goodness in your animal partner? We are all made by the same God from the same basic materials. There is a great universal unity and oneness in God's creation.

PRAYER: Thank you, LORD God for this common bond that we have with all creation. Amen.

GOD'S CREATION - OUR MANAGEMENT

Genesis 1:26-31 tells of God's creating humankind and of granting 'dominion' (lordship, oversight, stewardship, management, or overall care) of ***God's world.*** All creation **remains God's possession**. God grants to man and woman the holy responsibility and privilege to care for that which God has made.

All creation remains God's possession. God grants to man and woman the holy responsibility and privilege to care for that which God has made.

'[26]Then God said, "Let us make humankind in our image, according to our likeness; and *let them have dominion* over the fish of the sea, and over the birds of the air, and over the cattle, and over all the wild animals of the earth, and over every creeping thing that creeps upon the earth."'

DEVOTION: Partnering with a fellow creature of God is a holy and dedicated 'stewardship' privilege. It is truly a gift from God. How have you done in fulfilling your sacred responsibilities in the care and nurture of your animal friend? Have you provided shelter, food, water, and care? Have you protected your animal friend and given your love?

PRAYER: Help me to reflect your Divine love and care in my sacred companionship with my pet, Lord God. Amen.

For more on this topic, please read Genesis 1:26-31 and Proverbs 12:10.

QUOTE: "Of all God's creatures, there is only one that cannot be made slave of the lash. That one is the cat. If man could be crossed with the cat it would improve the man, but it would deteriorate the cat." - *Mark Twain*

QUOTE: "There are two means of refuge from the miseries of life: music and cats." - *Albert Schweitzer*

GOD RESCUES HUMANS AND ANIMALS - THE FLOOD

The Bible account of Noah and the ark is well known by many. It tells about how God saved Noah, his family and the animals in the ark. It is an illustration of God's continued care for *all* creation, not just for humanity.

God saved both the human and the animal kingdom from destruction in the waters of the great flood.

This is the sign of the covenant that I have established between me and all flesh...

- Genesis 9:17

Genesis 8:15-16

'[15]Then God said to Noah, [16]"Go out of the ark, you and your wife, and your sons and your sons' wives with you. [17]*Bring out with you every living thing that is with you of all flesh – birds and animals and every creeping thing that creeps on the earth – so that they may abound on the earth, and be fruitful and multiply on the earth.'"*

For more, please read all of Genesis Chapters 7 and 8.

QUOTE: "It wasn't raining when Noah built the ark." - *Howard Ruff*

DEVOTION: God saved humankind and the animals. God both created and saved this particular beloved animal friend just for you. Imagine that!

PRAYER: Thank you God for this gracious gift of companionship and the special friendship that you have made possible for us together. Amen.

GOD'S FIRST ETERNAL COVENANT – THE RAINBOW

Genesis 9:8-11, 16

God's first "eternal covenant" (or enduring holy promise) is to *all* living things. God promised to never again to destroy the earth by flood because of human sin. The "bow in the clouds" (rainbow) is to be taken as a sign of that eternal promise, not just to Noah and his descendants, but to *'all flesh.'*

'[8]Then God said to Noah and to his sons with him, [9]"As for me, I am
establishing my covenant with you and your descendants after you,[10]*and
with every living creature that is with you, the birds, the domestic animals, and
every animal of the earth with you, as many as came out of the ark.* [11]*I establish my
covenant with you, that never again shall all flesh be cut off by the waters of a
flood, and never again shall there be a flood to destroy the earth…*[16]When the bow
is in the clouds, I will see it and remember the everlasting covenant
between God and every living creature of all flesh that is on the earth."'

For some who have chosen to move beyond the Bible's clear intent – *God's rainbow has become a cultural symbol.* Some attach a hope of a life after death – one's passage from this life into everlasting life - to the sign of the rainbow. Clearly, the Bible does not make that connection either expressly or by implication. But some, in a leap of romantic visioning, imagine that this passage is where the 'rainbow bridge' and other similar eternity themed poetry originate. Please note: *there are Bible passages that clearly place animals and other creatures in heaven.* This passage is *not* one of them.

From the Bible's own perspective**, the rainbow is a lasting symbol of God's supreme love, mercy and care for all life.** Further, there is visual irony in a rainbow – of awe inspiring and surprising beauty in the midst of a storm. *The Biblical beauty of the rainbow is in God's holy promise.* God delivered Noah, his family and all the animals in the ark from destruction. God promises in the rainbow to never again 'cut off' or destroy the earth by a flood. Instead of a raging storm to destroy, God promises glorious colors in the clouds. That's both incredibly beautiful and romantic.

For more, please read all of Genesis chapter 9.

QUOTE: "Somewhere over the rainbow, skies are blue, and dreams that you dare to dream, really do come true." - *Lyman Frank Baum*

QUOTE: "May God give you…for every storm a rainbow, for every tear a smile, for every care a promise and a blessing in each trial. For every problem life send a faithful friend to share, for every sigh a sweet song and an answer for each prayer." - *Traditional Irish blessing*

DEVOTION: God rescues and saves all creation. God has given an eternal covenant to all living things with the rainbow. God promises to care for all that was made.

How have you partnered with God to care for your beloved animal friend?

PRAYER: Eternal God, you have given all living things your holy promise to save and rescue us. Hold all humans and animals in your Divine care, and use us for your sacred purposes to further Your Kingdom. Amen.

GOD COMMANDS ALL CREATION TO REST

The Ten Commandments are instructions to God's chosen people. People are to honor God as the owner of all and the giver of all good gifts. They are to respond in gratitude simply by following God's teaching. The instruction in the Ten Commandments about Sabbath Rest relates to both people and animals. Working animals and livestock were also to be given a rest. Here God's commands are not just for humans but apply to animals.

Exodus 20:8-11

"...you shall not do any work - you, your son or your daughter... your livestock..."

\- *Exodus 20:10*

"8Remember the Sabbath day, and
keep it holy. 9Six days you shall labor
and do all your work. 10But the seventh
day is a Sabbath to the LORD your God;
*you shall not do any work – you, your son or your daughter, your male or female slave, your livestock, or the alien resident in your towns.*11For in six days
the LORD made heaven and earth, the sea, and all that is in them, but rested the seventh day; therefore the LORD blessed the Sabbath day and consecrated it."

For more on the Ten Commandments, please read Exodus Chapter 20 and Deuteronomy Chapter 5.

QUOTE: "The greatness of a nation and its moral progress can be judged by the way its animals are treated." - *Mahatma Gandhi*

DEVOTION: God instructed the people of the covenant to honor Him in resting from labor, and to shape that Sabbath day for all within their oversight, including livestock and all animals. How have you cared and nurtured your dear companion?

How have you honored God in your care for all creation and in your observing the Sabbath rest?

PRAYER: Lord God, help us to pause to reflect on your Divine goodness in all things. Guide us into the ways of your truth. As you discipline and nurture us, direct us to shape our contact with our animals to be mutually supportive, caring and loving. Amen.

GOD AND CREATION IN THE PSALMS

God as both the Creator and Savior of all is a frequent theme in the Biblical Book of Psalms. The authors of the Psalms celebrate all creation praising the Eternal God in its own unique way. God's Lordship and care of creation undergirds many of these ancient hymns.

Psalm 36 contrasts the evil and wickedness of humanity with the mercy and astounding grace of the Eternal God. This hymn of praise then expresses the depth of God's steadfast love in verses 5-10 that follow. *This one particular scripture passage appears to give an undeniably clear answer,* **"Will our animal companions be in heaven?"** What do you think?

Psalm 36:5-10

"5 Your steadfast love, O Lord, extends to the heavens, your faithfulness to
the clouds. 6 Your righteousness is like the mighty mountains; your
judgments are like the great deep; *you save humans and animals alike, O Lord.*

7 How precious is your steadfast love, O God! All people may take refuge
in the shadow of your wings. 8 They feast on the abundance of your house,
and you give them drink from the river of your delights. 9 For with you is
the fountain of life; in your light we see light. 10 O continue your steadfast
love to those who know you and your salvation to the upright of heart!"

The original Hebrew verb used here is תושיע or rendered in English - yawsha.' The Hebrew word yawsha' means "to save." In total fairness, some modern English translations substitute 'preserve,' 'deliver,' 'rescue' or 'care' instead of "save," depending on the translators' inclinations. The Hebrew is most clear. In this passage God clearly "saves" both humans and animals alike.

For more on the theme of 'God and Creation,' please read Psalms 8, 50, 96, 104, 145, 148 and 150.

DEVOTION: God's steadfast love embraces all creation – absolutely everything. What God has created; God saves. What surprising, all encompassing and amazing love!

God is the ultimate owner of your animal companion, too. God has delegated you responsibility for that life and for its nurture and care. How are you reflecting God's 'steadfast' love – with your animal companion, with all creation and even with the rest of humankind?

PRAYER: Lord God, help me to reflect your wisdom, strength, nurture and steadfast loving character in my care all of your creation. Amen.

GOD CARES FOR US THROUGH ANIMALS

God is shown as Lord of all creation in sending animals to care for people. In this passage, God sends ravens to feed the prophet Elijah and care for him in a time of famine.

1 Kings 17:5-6

"So he [Elijah] went and did according to the word of the LORD…[6]The ravens brought him bread and meat in the morning, and bread and meat in the evening…"

DEVOTION: In how many ways has your animal companion cared for you? Can you even begin to count the ways? Can you not see the hand of a loving God providing for your needs through your pet?

In our home, our dog Calee was our little four-pawed therapist. She instinctively knew who needed a little extra affection and love on any given day. She showed us unselfish and sometimes sacrificial support. We came to see her care as 'God's whisper of love.' She reflected God's love.

PRAYER: With you, O Lord, all are one. You made us to care and nurture each other. Help me to see your love and care reflected in my animal friend. Amen.

For more on God caring or working to save humanity through animals, read Jonah 2:1-11 and Numbers 22. For the wisdom found in animals, read Job 12:7-10.

GOD'S GIFT OF HOPE - THE PEACEABLE KINGDOM

In the Old Testament **Book of Isaiah**, the Israelites were suffering torment as slaves in Babylon. They desperately needed some Divine message of hope. Chapter 11 is a passage about God, humanity and all the creatures of God's world. It is a message of hope from God for all creation.

Isaiah 11: The Peaceable Kingdom

"The wolf shall live with the lamb: the leopard shall lie down with the kid..."

- Isaiah 11:6

"6 The wolf shall live with the lamb,
the leopard shall lie down with the kid,
the calf and the lion and the fatling
together, and a little child shall lead them.
7 The cow and the bear shall graze,
their young shall lie down together;
and the lion shall eat straw like the ox.
8 The nursing child shall play over the hole
of the asp and the weaned child shall put
its hand on the adder's den.
9 They will not hurt or destroy on all my

holy mountain; for the earth will be full of the knowledge of the LORD as the waters cover the sea."

QUOTE: "The wolf and the lamb shall feed together, and the lion shall eat straw like the bullock: and dust shall be the serpent's meat. They shall not hurt nor destroy in all my holy mountain, declares the LORD."
- Isaiah 65:25

DEVOTION: Can you see a glimmer of God's eternal message of peace and everlasting hope through your beloved animal friend?

My wife Lee went through chemotherapy in 2004 and was often fully exhausted by her treatments. It was during this critical health episode that our dog lay next to her literally all day long to bring her comfort, peace and companionship. Lee could well say that they went through the cancer treatment together – and Calee became a very welcome part of God's healing grace.

PRAYER: God of all time, at the last you will renew all creation – human and animal - and all will be at peace.

Create in me that Peace which passes all human understanding. Let me be a bringer of Peace to those around me. Amen.

For more on our need for God's 'Peaceable kingdom,' please read all of Isaiah Chapter 11 and Hosea 4:1-6.

GOD'S COVENANT TO ALL CREATION

The prophet Hosea called the people back to a holy relationship with God. In Chapter 2 the animal kingdom is included in God's promises. Here we clearly see that God's promises are for all living things.

Hosea 2:18

"[18]I will make for you a covenant on that day with the wild animals, the birds of the air, and the creeping things of the ground; and I will abolish the bow, the sword, and war from the land; and I will make you lie down in safety."

DEVOTION: Oh, for a moment of peace! Do you see how God cares for all creation, human and animal, alike? Those precious moments with your animal companion may bring a small peek into God's eternity – peace.

Jesus said, "Peace I leave you. God's peace I give you; not as the world gives, give I unto you. Let not your hearts be troubled, neither let them be afraid. It is the Father's good pleasure to give you the Kingdom."
- John 14:27

PRAYER: Thank you, O Lord for your gift of eternal peace for all. Amen.

GOD AND ANIMALS IN THE NEW TESTAMENT

GOD USES A ROOSTER AS A WITNESS

Maybe you remember this story. Jesus was sharing the Passover meal with his disciples in an Upper Room in Jerusalem. On that occasion he told Simon (Peter) that he would deny knowing Jesus three times before the cock (rooster) crowed. Peter strongly rejected that possibility. Yet as the story unfolds, that is exactly what happens. Although not a story about a rooster, God used this call of the animal world to summon Simon to repent.

Mark 14:27-31 and 71-72 - Peter's Denial Foretold

"27And Jesus said to them, 'You will all become deserters...' 29Peter said to
him, 'Even though all become deserters, I will not.' 30Jesus said to him,
*'Truly I tell you, this day, this very night, before the cock crows twice, you will
deny me three times.'* 31But he said vehemently, 'Even though I must die with
you, I will not deny you.' And all of them said the same."

Peter Denies Jesus

"71But he began to curse, and he swore an oath, 'I do not know this man
you are talking about.'72At that moment the cock crowed for the second
time. Then Peter remembered that Jesus had said to him, *'Before the cock
crows twice, you will deny me three times.' And he broke down and wept.*"

DEVOTION: How often do our animal companions remind us of God's mercy *and* love – and of our human failures? Peter repented of his failure; he was forgiven and restored. This has always been God's intent. Have you permitted God to restore you to wholeness and holiness?

PRAYER: Help me, O God in my weakness and human frailty. Forgive me and restore me to that holy relationship you desire for me and all creation. Amen.

For more on this story, please read all of Mark Chapter 14.

For more on this topic, see also Matthew 10:29-31 and Matthew 21:1-11.

JESUS TEACHES ABOUT GOD'S CARE FOR CREATION

Matthew 6:25-30 - Do Not Worry

"[25] Therefore I tell you, do not worry about your life, what you will eat or
what you will drink, or about your body, what you will wear. Is not life
more than food, and the body more than clothing? [26]*Look at the birds of the*
air; they neither sow nor reap nor gather into barns, and yet your heavenly Father
feeds them. Are you not of more value than they? [27]And can any of you by
worrying add a single hour to your span of life? [28]And why do you worry
about clothing? *Consider the lilies of the field, how they grow; they neither toil*

nor spin, [29]*yet I tell you, even Solomon in all*
his glory was not clothed like one of these. [30]But
if God so clothes the grass of the field, which is alive today and tomorrow is thrown into the oven, will he not much more clothe you—you of little faith."

Look at the birds of the air: they neither sow nor reap nor gather into barns, and yet your heavenly Father feeds them.

- *Matthew 6:26*

For more read Matthew 6:25-34

DEVOTION: Jesus taught about God's holy desire for all creation. In response to people worrying about the uncertainties of the future and things that were beyond their control, he used the animal and plant realm as an example of God's benevolent care - and especially of God's care for humankind and their needs. God cares about all of nature - *and God loves YOU*!

PRAYER: Be my Rock and my Strong Foundation, O Lord. In you I place my trust. Amen.

QUOTE: "God gives every bird its food, but He does not throw it into its nest." - *J. G. Holland.*

GOD'S NEW CREATION

The Book of Revelation is about the end times and final things. It is about God, who is the beginning and end. It is about God's promise to make all things new, perfect in every way, without the blemishes caused by sin and our separation from God. Everything will be restored, new and perfect.

It is a book written in rich literary code for a faithful people suffering under severe persecution. This 'revelation' was given to John on the island of Patmos. He chose to faithfully record what was revealed to him.

CREATURES IN HEAVEN: **Revelation 5:11-14**

"11 Then I looked, and I heard the voice of many angels surrounding the
throne and *the living creatures* and the elders; they numbered myriads of
myriads and thousands of thousands, 12 singing with full voice, 'Worthy is
the Lamb that was slaughtered to receive power and wealth and wisdom
and might and honor and glory and blessing!'
13 Then I heard *every creature in heaven and on earth and under the earth and in*
the sea, and all that is in them, singing, 'To the one seated on the throne and to the
Lamb be blessing and honor and glory and might for ever and ever!'
14 And the four living creatures said,
'Amen!' And the elders fell down and
worshipped."

> *Then I heard every creature in heaven and on earth... singing...*
>
> \- *Revelation 5:13*

DEVOTION: As the heavenly scroll is unsealed in Revelation 5, all of heaven praises God and sings. There clearly are many creatures in heaven.

Can you imagine your beloved animal friends there, too - meowing, barking, chirping, in their own unique voices, singing the praises of the everlasting and majestic God?

PRAYER: Into your eternal arms we commend all for whom we pray, trusting in your mercy, through Jesus Christ our Lord. Amen.

QUOTE: "Be thou comforted little dog. Thou too in Resurrection shall have a little golden tail." - attributed to *Martin Luther*

GOD'S PERFECT KINGDOM

Revelation 21 is the final vision of God's new perfect world. For people of faith - life is about God's goodness. So, the vision of God's new heaven and new earth includes ALL THINGS. This 'all things' refers to all of God's original creation.

The New Heaven and the New Earth

REVELATION 21:1, 5 "Then I saw *a new heaven and a new earth*…[5] And the one who was seated on the throne said, 'See, I am making *all things* new.'"

What do you envision when you contemplate the phrase, "all things new?" The original Greek wording here is all-encompassing – pan'tah - "Ἰδοὺ καινὰ ποιῶ **πάντα**". **Πάντα** (pan'tah) means quite literally "everything." English language Bible versions translate this as 'all things' or 'everything.'

For more, please read all of Revelation 21.

DEVOTION: Imagine your beloved animal friends included in the "all things" in the previous passage, and in so doing, give thanks for God's Divine purpose and loving kindness.

God will dwell with all the faithful people; God will be with us and all things in this 'eternity.'

Are you able to comprehend that God's promises may apply to the whole creation, including you and your beloved animal companions?

PRAYER: Lord, you promise to make all things new. Begin with me today, and my life will show forth your praise and goodness! Amen.

For more, please read John 1:1-4, Mark 16:15, Luke 12:6 and Colossians 1:15-20.

QUOTE: "In spite of the way many people are turning away from God, not for other gods, but for no god; in spite of the mess we are making of this beautiful Planet Earth which God has given us, God still loves the world." - *Eva Burrows*

QUOTE: (The Eleventh Commandment) "You shall not despoil the earth and the life thereon." – *Sterling E. Lanier* (quoted from Hiero's Journey).

GOD'S CREATION CELEBRATED IN HYMNS

In public worship over the past few weeks I've been struck by just how much of the Church's sacred music speaks about all God's creatures and the glory of creation. These songs either thank God for creation – or celebrate the oneness of all creation (all living things, water, earth, sky…) praising the Eternal God.

Here is an alphabetical list of Creation hymns that I recommend:

All Creatures of Our God and King

All Things Bright and Beautiful

All You Works of God

Creating God, Your Finger Trace

Earth and All Stars

Fairest Lord Jesus

For all the Saints

For the Beauty of the Earth

From all that Dwell below the Skies

Glorious Things of Thee are Spoken

God of the Sparrow, God of the Whale

God, who Stretched the Spangled Heavens

Great is Thy Faithfulness

Here I am Lord

His Eye is on the Sparrow

Holy, Holy, Holy, Lord God Almighty

How Great Thou Art

How Marvelous God's Greatness

I am His and He is Mine

I am the Bread of Life

Immortal, Invisible God Only Wise

I Sing a Song of the Saints of God

I Sing the Almighty Power of God

I, The Lord of Sea and Sky

I was There to Hear your Borning Cry

Jesus is Coming Again

Jesus Shall Reign Where'er the Sun

Joyful, Joyful We Adore Thee

Let All on Earth their Voices Raise

Let All the World in Every Corner Sing

Let All Things Now Living

Let There be Peace on Earth

Lift Every Voice and Sing

Many, Great God, Are Your Works

Morning Has Broken

My God is There Controlling

O All Ye Works of God Now Come

O Day of Rest and Gladness

O Worship the King all Glorious

On Eagle's Wings

Praise and Thanksgiving, Father We Offer

Praise God, from Whom All Blessings Flow (Doxology)

Praise to the Lord, the King of Creation

Praise We the Lord

Shout to the Lord

Sing Out, Earth and Skies

Sing to God with Gladness, all Creation

Teach Us What We Yet May Be

The Heavens Declare Thy Glory

This is My Father's World

We Bow Down

We Sing the Greatness of Our God

When Long Before Time

When Morning Guilds the Skies

Doxology

DEVOTION: With God, all creation is one. With many voices, all creation sings one song of God's goodness. This is a message of comfort for those who have a measure of affection and care for the creatures in God's world; those who strive to be upright and without blame before God.

PRAYER: Eternal God, you create and breathe existence to all that lives. At the last receive us all – human and animal - into your all-sustaining care, within your Divine mercy. Amen.

BIBLE LEARNING SUMMARY

- God created everything. We are all made from the same common elements by the same Divine Creator.

- All creation remains God's possession. We have a holy responsibility to care for all God has made.

- God rescued both humans and animals within the ark from the great flood.

- God gave the first eternal covenant to 'all flesh,' with the rainbow as the enduring sign of God's promise.

- God instructed people of faith and the animals in their care to observe a Sabbath Rest.

In the Psalms, God - in his steadfast love - saves both animals and humankind, alike.

God offers care to people through animals.

God gave a vision of people, animals and all creation living in peace.

God employs animals to remind people of Divine mercy and love.

Jesus used flowers and birds to illustrate the value of all creation to God.

In God's eternity, there are visions of all creatures and all creation restored to perfection and at peace – all praising God.

The Church's worship regularly celebrates all creation praising God.

SPACE FOR YOUR NOTES:

QUOTE: "How we behave toward cats here below determines our status in heaven." - *Robert A. Heinlein* [The same might be justly said for all creatures.]

QUOTE: "I care not much for a man's religion whose dog and cat are not the better for it. " - *Abraham Lincoln*

God consistently shows love and care for all creation, not just humans. God has rescued and saved the animals from destruction. God has promised to restore all things to an eternal perfection – a new heaven and a new earth. God is God; we are not. God loves all creation and life. God made this world and all its creatures - a marvelous array of animals and plants, birds and fish. Thus, how can we limit our imagination and vision that God's eternity and all that God finally determines to be there will be somehow greatly different?

For a full summary of Bible passages that are cited, please see page 57.

DEVOTIONALS ABOUT ANIMALS

SAINT FRANCIS OF ASSISI – PATRON SAINT OF ALL ANIMALS

Saint Francis, Assisi, was known for his special connection to animals and his devotion for all God's creation. Thus, he is known as the **Patron Saint of animals and ecology**. He adopted Jesus' words in **Mark 16:15**, **'**15And he said to them, "Go into all the world and proclaim the good news to the whole creation."' *The feast of St. Francis, Assisi, is October 4.*

A PRAYER OF SAINT FRANCIS

Lord, make me an instrument of your peace;
Where there is hatred, let me sow love;
Where there is injury, pardon:
Where there is doubt, faith;
Where there is despair, hope,
Where there is darkness, light,
Where there is sadness, joy.
O divine Master, grant that I may not so much seek to be consoled as to console;
To be understood, as to understand;
To be loved, as to love;
For it is in giving that we receive,
It is in pardoning that we are pardoned,
And it is in dying that we are born to Eternal Life. Amen.

RITE FOR THE BLESSING OF ANIMALS

"Blessed are you, Lord God, maker of all living creatures. You called forth fish in the sea, birds in the air and animals on the land. You inspired St. Francis to call all of them his brothers and sisters. We ask you to bless this pet. By the power of your love, enable it to live according to your plan. May we always praise you for all your beauty in your creation. Blessed are you, Lord our God, in all your creatures! *Amen.*"

HYMN – (Here a creation song or other hymn may be sung or read. Please see a list of hymn titles, pages 32-33.)

THE BLESSING PRAYER

All:
Most high, Almighty Lord, our Creator, yours are the praise, the glory, the honor and all blessings! All things were made and belong to you. You are to be praised for giving us the animals, birds and fish which fill your world. May we think of you and thank you when we play with and care for our animal companion. You are to be praised for making us filled with joy to have them to share love and affection. We ask you, Lord, that we may always be good to our pets, so that they may also be filled with joy. Help us to keep them in good health. O God, your world is wonderful. May we all come into your even greater world of the kingdom of heaven, where we shall see even more wonderful things and where we shall live and love forever. This we ask to your eternal praise, and to our blessing. *Amen.*

Hear our prayer O Lord ... for animals that are overworked, underfed, and cruelly treated; for all wistful creatures in captivity that beat their wings against bars; for any that are hunted or lost or deserted or frightened or hungry; for all that must be put to death.... and for those who deal with them we ask a heart of compassion and gentle hands and kindly words. Make us, ourselves, to be true friends to animals, and so to share the blessings of the merciful. *Amen.*

- *Albert Schweitzer*

PRAYERS FOR ANIMALS

O God, who has made all the earth and every creature that dwells therein: Help us, we pray you, to treat with compassion the living creatures entrusted to our care, that they may not suffer from our neglect nor become the victims of any cruelty; and grant that in caring for them we may find a deeper understanding of your love for all creation; through Jesus Christ our Lord. *Amen.*

We give you thanks, most gracious God, for the beauty of earth, sky and sea; for the richness of mountains, plains, and rivers; for the songs of birds and the loveliness of flowers. We praise you for these good gifts, and pray that we may safeguard them for our posterity. Grant that we may continue to grow in our grateful enjoyment of your abundant creation, to your honor and glory, now and forever. *Amen.*

O merciful Creator, your hand is open wide to satisfy the needs of every living creature: Make us always thankful for your loving care; and grant that we, remembering the account that we must one day give, may be faithful stewards of your good gifts; through Jesus Christ our Lord, who with you and the Holy Spirit lives and reigns, one God, forever and ever. *Amen.*

O God - who made everything good, teach us to love what you have made. Help us to see your creative impulse in the stars and planets, the trees and flowers, the rocks and the rivers, and especially in these precious animal companions you have entrusted to our care. How great is your name, O Lord our God, throughout all creation. *Amen.*

Lord God, you have made all living things, and you are even more wonderful than the things you have made. We thank you for giving us our pets who are our friends and who give us so much joy in life. We cherish the pets we have now, and we remember with gratitude the pets we have loved and lost. May we always be reminded of the joy we have shared together. May we, likewise, realize that as our pets trust us to take care of them, so we should trust you to take care of us, and in our taking care of them we may share in your love for all your creatures. Grant this through Christ our Lord. *Amen.*

PRAYERS FOR LOST PETS

Blessed are you, O Lord our God, for all living creatures you have made. You keep them in your care and not one of them is ever lost from your sight. They glorify you, each in its own way, and speak to us of your beauty and love. Bless them now and keep them from harm. They unquestionably accept their place in the rhythm of your creation. May we respect them and cherish them for they are your gift to us; through them may we come to know you better and praise you, their Creator. Blessed be the love and joy that they bring to us. *Amen.*

Eternal God, we appeal now for (name) who is lost. Guard and protect him / her from all fear. At the last, bring her / him safely to the end of the day, in heaven or in earth. Grant Your Divine peace and comfort now to this human family as they face the uncertain days ahead.

Keep watch with us, Lord God, with those who work, watch or weep this night. Give your holy angels charge over those who sleep and rest from their labors. Tend the sick, Lord Jesus, give rest to the weary, bless the dying, soothe the suffering, pity the afflicted, shield the joyous, all for your love's sake. *Amen.*

CEREMONY FOR RECEIVING A NEW PET

Hosea 2:18 – "I will make a covenant for you on that day with the wild animals, the birds of the air, and the creeping things of the ground; and I will abolish the bow, the sword and war from the land; and I will make you lie down in safety."

Lord God, you have created all things and given us the sacred responsibility for their care. We come to you this day to renew our pledge and promise of fidelity for those creatures you have placed among us. We pray that our nurture and love might reflect your Creative Love which has made and now sustains all things.

Grant us an abundant share of your peace and Divine Spirit that we may be united and one with all creation. By this act of affirmation bind us to you and our pet, as – in you - all are one.

Leader - What will you name your pet?

Response - (The name of the animal is given.)

Leader - I charge you to care for (name) as a holy creation of God.

Response - I willingly accept that responsibility and privilege.

Leader - I charge you to protect (name), be faithful and kind.

Response - I will, and ask God to help and guide me in His mercy and grace.

[As appropriate, the new family touches, pats, or strokes the animal as a sign of the promises they have now made.]

CLOSING CHARGE: May the Eternal God, who in the New Covenant in Christ Jesus gave us the grace to begin again and be restored, now assist you in showing mercy and compassion to all of God's creatures, even as God has shown us mercy. *Amen.*

PRAYER FOR ADOPTING A NEW PET

Creator God, we ask your blessings for this precious one that has now joined a new family. We pray that you bless this marvelous creation of yours, so that it may reflect a measure of your unconditional love and joy into this world. We ask that this pet be able to bring your love to this family.

We pray that this family will always be able to provide a nurturing, secure and loving home for this dear one and that their time together be blessed with the length of days as well as shared joy and love. In Jesus' name we ask this blessing. *Amen.*

PRAYER FOR A SICK ANIMAL

Eternal God, you hold all creation in the love of your Divine Care. In Jesus Christ you came among us to heal the sick, raise up the fallen and renew your people. He gave hope to those without hope. Our Lord Jesus identified with the outcast, homeless, vulnerable and the poor. He cast out evil and ushered in your Divine Kingdom of everlasting peace and justice for all creation.

As Christ cared for the human poor, sick, needy and outcast, now we lift up our appeal for our beloved creatures that are sick and in need. We especially pray for those creatures who may suffer through no fault of their own. Visit us now with your love and compassion and have mercy on our beloved (name) for whom we pray.

(The care giver may tenderly lay hands on the pet, as appropriate.)

May the Eternal Creator God free you from pain.

May God in his wisdom and mercy restore you to health.

May you at last be made complete and whole in God's perfect kingdom, under God's loving and tender care. *Amen.*

PRAYER FOR AGING PETS

Loving God, we pray for this dear one that has been with us for so long. Grant your blessing – that now may be your Divine and holy comfort as their time draws to a close.

We would desire that they are able to stay in their home with their familiar things and with their human family that they so love until that end time comes.

We pray that, although they are aging now and draw closer to their time left here in this physical world, they would be free from pain and suffering and that they will continue to experience the fullness of our joy and our love.

We ask your blessings that the remaining time with us is one of quiet love and peaceful companionship. When that end time comes that they are called home, we pray that you would receive them in the arms of your loving embrace.

Thank you, LORD God, for the time you have given us with our dear companion and for your grace in allowing our pet to stay so long here on

this earth and to be a blessing in our lives.
In Jesus' name, we ask these things. *Amen.*

PRAYER FOR A DEAD OR DYING PET

REVELATION 21

"Then I saw a new heaven and a new earth; for the first heaven and the
first earth had passed away, and the sea was no more. 2And I saw the holy
city, the New Jerusalem, coming down out of heaven from God, prepared
as a bride adorned for her husband. 3And I heard a loud voice from the
throne saying,
'See, the home of God is among mortals.
He will dwell with them;
they will be his peoples,
and God himself will be with them;
4he will wipe every tear from their eyes.
Death will be no more;
mourning and crying and pain will be no more,
for the first things have passed away.'

And the one who was seated on the throne said, *'See, I am making all things new.'* Also he said, 'Write this, for these words are trustworthy and true.'
6Then he said to me, 'It is done! I am the Alpha and the Omega, the
beginning and the end.' "

PRAYER: Eternal God, we know that you embrace all things, time and all eternity. Every living thing is yours and will return to you. Creator God – your world is fragile and precious are all your creatures.

We remember in thanksgiving the life of (name) that you shared with us. We now commend (name) to your loving embrace.

Grant us renewed senses to hear, see, touch and know how all of creation speaks of your love. Give us a dedicated impulse to protect and defend your creation and sing of your glory. Create again within us a holy sense of gratitude for your gift to us of (name) who has shared this life with us and freely shared love and affection.

In our grief and sorrow, give us reason to rejoice for the awareness that all creation and creatures are of your making – and that by your grace, we may live again together in your holy, new and perfect kingdom. *Amen.*

LITURGY FOR THE BURIAL OF A PET

(This family service may be adapted as local circumstances dictate. The symbol N. indicates where either the PET'S or OWNER'S NAME is to be inserted.)

A Service of celebration and remembrance for N (pet).

Leader: "Blessed be the God and Father of our Lord Jesus Christ, the Creator of us all; our Holy God who is LORD of all is a gentle and compassionate God who comforts us in our sorrows so that we can comfort others in their sorrows with the consolation we ourselves have received from God." (2 Corinthians 1:3-4)

Response: Thanks be to God.

Leader: Psalm 121

1 I lift up my eyes to the hills—
from where will my help come?
2 My help comes from the Lord,
who made heaven and earth.

3 He will not let your foot be moved;
he who keeps you will not slumber.

4He who keeps Israel
will neither slumber nor sleep.

5The Lord is your keeper;
the Lord is your shade at your right hand.
6The sun shall not strike you by day, nor the moon by night.

7The Lord will keep you from all evil;
he will keep your life.
8The Lord will keep
your going out and your coming in
from this time on and for evermore.

READER: "And if one's heart be straight with God, then every creature shall be to you a mirror of life and a book of holy doctrine, for there is no creature so little or so vile, but that shows and represents the goodness of God." - Thomas à Kempis (1380-1471) *German monk, devotional author.*

"Not to hurt our humble [animal] brethren is our first duty to them, but to stop there is not enough. We have a higher mission - to be of service to them wherever they require it." St. Francis of Assisi

LEADER: In Holy Scripture, our Lord Jesus taught that even the needs of the common birds of the field are known by You, LORD God. We thank you for N., and for the dear companionship he / she brought us. We thank you for all of your creation that surrounds us and the pets who continue to share our home.

Comfort us now in our grief and loss of a dear friend. We know that you share our grief and offer us hope. We implore now the granting of your Divine peace, in the knowledge that you hold all things in your eternal love. Bring us all at last to your eternal kingdom, where we all long to be united before your throne of grace; through Jesus Christ our Lord. *Amen.*

LEADER: Our Lord Jesus, who for us is the Good Shepherd of all the sheep, now enfold us with His love, walk by our side, give us eternal hope and fill us with everlasting peace. *Amen.*

(Other hymns may be sung or recited. Please, see hymns on pages 32-33.)

PRAYERS FOR CATS
SAINT GERTRUDE, PATRON SAINT OF CATS

St Gertrude, former Abbess of Nivelles, Brabant, died in the year 659 and is patron saint of cats and gardeners.

"YE SHALL NOT POSSESS ANY BEAST, MY DEAR SISTERS, SAVE ONLY A CAT..." – St. Gertrude

The feast of St. Gertrude, Nivelles is March 17

CAT OWNER'S PRAYER

Because I'm only human,
It's sometimes hard to be
The wise, all-knowing creature
That my cat expects of me.

And so I pray for special help
To somehow understand
The subtle implications
Of each proud meowed command.

Oh, let me not forget that chairs
Were put on earth to shred;
And what I like to call a lap
Is actually a bed.

I know it's really lots to ask
But please, oh please, take pity;
And though I'm only human,
Make me worthy of my kitty!

- Author Unknown

A CAT'S PRAYER

(Fleur Puss)

Thank you, God, for harvest-time,
For milk, for meat, for fish,
Thank you, God, for all the food,
I find upon my dish.

Thank you, God, for Autumn time,
When leaves come tumbling down,
Thank you for their pretty colors,
Red, and gold, and brown.

Thank you, God, for giving me,
A lovely coat of fur,
Thank you, God, that I can talk
By means of mew and purr.

Thank you for my happy home,
Where love and care abound;
Thank you for its warmth and comfort,
Always to be found.

Thank you, God, for all the gifts,
That life has given me;
Dear God, who made us all, I raise
My humble paws to Thee.

THE CAT'S CAROL

(Sister Letitia)

Tune: Once In Royal David's City

Come you cats of every color
Kittens, too, of every size
See, the Lord who made the tiger
Lowly in a manger lies.
Praise him all his little tigers
Let your joyful purring rise.

Siamese and stately Persian
Homely black and Tabby gray,
Leave your cushions, leave your roof tops
Call a truce with mice today.
Swift and silent, velvet footed
Hasten now down Bethlehem way.

See, he smiles to see you coming
Mary welcomes you within.
Joseph with a friendly finger
Gently strokes your furry chin.
Ox and ass are there beside you
Sheep and camel peering in.
All creation sings his praises
Voices, music, sharps and flats
Join the chorus, cats and kittens
Praise him, just by being cats.

PRAYERS FOR DOGS

SAINT ROCH, PATRON SAINT OF DOGS

"The least we owe them is to lead a life worthy of their devotion."

The feast of St. Roch is August 16.

A DOG'S PRAYER FOR HIS OWNER

O Lord of humans, make my master faithful to his fellow men as I am to him. Grant that he may be as devoted to his friends and family as I am to him.

May he be open-faced and undeceptive as I am; may he be true to trust reposed in him as I am.

Give him a face cheerful like unto my wagging tail. Give him a spirit of gratitude like unto my flicking tongue.

Fill him with patience like unto mine that awaits his footsteps uncomplaining for hours. Fill him with my watchfulness, my courage, and my readiness to sacrifice comfort or life itself.

Keep him always young in heart and endowed with the spirit of play, as I am.

Make him as good a person as I am a dog. And make him worthy of me, his dog. *Amen.* (- Author unknown)

A POLICE DOG'S PRAYER

Oh Almighty God,
whose great power and eternal wisdom embraces the universe, watch over my handler while I sleep. Protect my handler from harm while I am unable to do so. I pray, help keep our streets and homes safe while my handler and I rest. I ask for your loving care because my handler's duty is dangerous.
Grant my handler your unending strength and courage in our daily assignments.

Dear God, protect my brave handler, grant your almighty protection, unite my handler safely with the family after the tour of duty has ended. I ask nothing for myself.
Amen.

(Author - Unknown)

GOD AND DOG

God summoned a beast from the field and He said, "Behold man, created in my image. Therefore adore him. You shall protect him in the wilderness, shepherd his flocks, watch over his children, and accompany him wherever he may go - even unto civilization. You shall be his companion, his ally, his slave."

"To do these things," God said, "I endow you with these instincts uncommon to other beasts: faithfulness, devotion, and understanding surpassing those of man himself. Lest it impair your courage, you shall never foresee your death. Lest it impair your loyalty, you shall be blind to the faults of man. Lest it impair your understanding, you are denied the power of words. Let no fault of language cleave an accord beyond that of man with any other beast - or even man with man. Speak to your master only with your mind, and through your honest eyes.

Walk by his side; sleep in his doorway; forage for him, ward off his enemies, carry his burdens, share his afflictions; love him and comfort him. And in return for this, man will fulfill your needs and wants - which shall be only food, shelter, and affection.

So be silent, and be a friend to man. Guide him through the perils along the way to the land that I have promised him. This shall be your destiny and your immortality." So spake the Lord.

And the dog heard and was content. (Author Unknown)

FOR ALL PETS – "A LIVING LOVE"

If you ever love an animal, **there are three days in your life you will always remember . . .**

The first is a day, blessed with happiness, when you bring home your young new friend. You may have spent weeks deciding on a breed. You may have asked numerous opinions of many vets, or done long research in finding a breeder. Or, perhaps in a fleeting moment, you may have just chosen that silly looking mutt in a shelter -- simply because something in its eyes reached your heart. But when you bring that chosen pet home, and watch it explore, and claim its special place in your hall or front room -- and when you feel it brush against you for the first time -- it instills a feeling of pure love you will carry with you through the many years to come.

The second day will occur eight or nine or ten years later. It will be a day like any other. Routine and unexceptional. But, for a surprising instant, you will look at your longtime friend and see age where you once saw youth. You will see slow deliberate steps where you once saw energy. And you will see sleep when you once saw activity. So you will begin to adjust your friend's diet -- and you may add a pill or two to her food. And you may feel a growing fear deep within yourself, which bodes of a coming emptiness. And you will feel this uneasy feeling, on and off, **until the third day finally arrives.**

And on this day -- if your friend and whatever higher being you believe in have not decided for you, then you will be faced with making a decision of your own -- on behalf of your lifelong friend, and with the guidance of your own deepest Spirit. But whichever way your friend eventually leaves you -- you will feel as alone as a single star in the dark night.

If you are wise, you will let the tears flow as freely and as often as they must. And if you are typical, you will find that not many in your circle of family or friends will be able to understand your grief, or comfort you.

But if you are true to the love of the pet you cherished through the many joy-filled years, you may find that a soul - a bit smaller in size than your own - seems to walk with you, at times, during the lonely days to come.

And at moments when you least expect anything out of the ordinary to happen, you may feel something brush against your leg – very, very lightly.

And looking down at the place where your dear, perhaps dearest friend used to lie - you will remember those three significant days. The memory will most likely be painful, and leave an ache in your heart.

As time passes the ache will come and go as if it has a life of its own. You will both reject it and embrace it, and it may confuse you. If you reject it, it will depress you. If you embrace it, it will deepen you. Either way, it will still be an ache.

But there will be, I assure you, **a fourth day** when - along with the memory of your pet - and piercing through the heaviness in your heart - there will come a realization that belongs only to you. It will be as unique and strong as our relationship with each animal we have loved, and lost. **This realization takes the form of a Living Love** - like the heavenly scent of a rose that remains after the petals have wilted, this Love will remain and grow -- and be there for us to remember. It is a love we have earned. It is the legacy our pets leave us when they go. And it is a gift we may keep with us as long as we live. It is a Love which is ours alone. And until we ourselves leave, perhaps to join our Beloved Pets -- it is a Love we will always possess. - *Martin Scot Kosins*

PETS' LOVE

A companion, a pal,
A very best friend.
Someone to trust,
To love 'til the end.
Someone to trust,
When feeling blue.

Always a smile,
T'always greet you.
Always a smile,
To dry up your tears.
A person to be there,
To quiet your fears.

A person to be there,
When lonely or sad.
Loving regardless,
If hating or mad.
Loving regardless,
If caring or cruel.
No matter what,
Genius or fool.

No matter what,
They stand by you.
Who is this person?
Have you a clue?
Who is this person?
I'll tell you who.
This is your pet,
That loves through 'n through.

(Author – Unknown)

INDEX OF NOTABLE QUOTES

Baum, Lyman Frank 16

Burrows, Eva................................ 31

Gandhi, Mahatma......................... 18

Genesis 3:8 9

Graham, Billy 7

Heinlein, Robert 36

Holland, J. G.................................27

Kempis, Thomas à 47

Kosins, Martin Scot 55

Lanier, Sterling E..........................31

Letitia, Sister................................50

Lincoln, Abraham 36

Luther, Martin...............................29

Rogers, Will...................................7

Ruff, Howard 14

Saint Francis 38, 47

Saint Gertrude...............................48

Saint Roch 51

Schweitzer, Albert 10, 13, 39

Traditional Irish Blessing 16

Twain, Mark 13

Unknown…………... ...... 52, 53, 55

INDEX OF BIBLE PASSAGES

(Listed in Biblical order)

Genesis 1:1-25 10

Genesis 1:26-31........................... 12

Genesis 3:19................................. 9

Genesis 7 and 8 14

Genesis 9...................................... 15

Genesis 20:8-11 17

Deuteronomy 5............................ 17

Numbers 22.................................. 22

1 Kings 17:5-6............................. 21

Job 12:7-10.................................. 22

Psalm 8.. 20

Psalm 36...................................... 19

Psalm 50...................................... 20

Psalm 96...................................... 20

Psalm 104.................................... 20

Psalm 121.................................... 46

Psalm 145.................................... 20

Psalm 148.................................... 20

Psalm 150............................20

Proverbs 12:10.............................12

Ecclesiastes 3:16-22 9

Isaiah 11:1-29 22

Isaiah 65:25 23

Hosea 2:18 .... 24, 42

Hosea 4:1-6..................................24

Jonah 2:1-11 22

Matthew 6:25-34 26

Matthew 10:29-31 26

Matthew 21:1-11 26

Mark 14:26-72..............................25

Mark 16:15 .... 30, 37

Luke 12:6.....................................30

John 1:1-4 30

John 14:27 24

Colossians 1:15-29 30

Revelation 5:11-14 28

Revelation 21:1-7 .... 30, 45

PAGE FOR NOTES OR PHOTOS

PAGE FOR NOTES OR PHOTOS

ABOUT THE AUTHOR

The Rev'd Dr. Neal Otto Hively is an ordained Evangelical Lutheran Church in America clergyman. He has served parishes in south central Pennsylvania, and as Senior Pastor of Trinity Evangelical Lutheran Church, Chambersburg, PA since 1994.

He has published works relating to Pennsylvania Original Land Records for York, Adams and Franklin counties. See www.paland.us for Dr. Hively's website for PA original colonial land.

He is married to Lee Codd of Bel Air, Maryland. They have two grown children, Christopher and Beth Ellen.

In the spring 2010 the Hively's Maltese dog Calee died. Their veterinarian inquired if Dr. Hively was aware of any published work that would answer the question, "Do animals go to heaven?" Pets and Heaven is a result of that inquiry and is now commended to the reader - to determine their own more informed conclusion to that question.

THANK YOU to the many friends who assisted in reviewing this work to offer helpful suggestions and kind wishes.

Sol Gloria Dei: To the Glory of God alone.